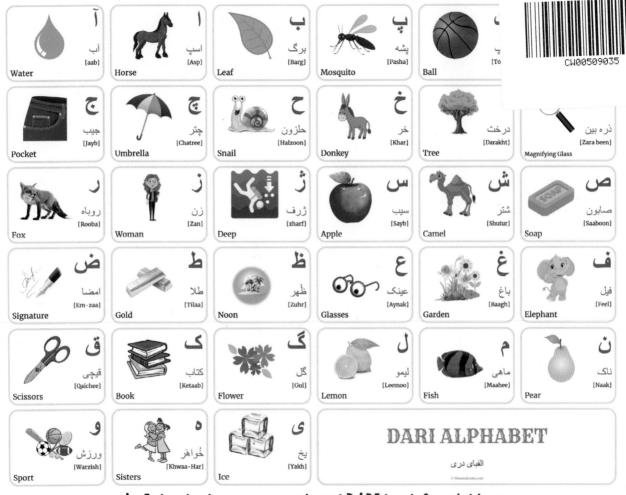

آ آب [aab] **Water**	ا اسپ [Asp] **Horse**	ب برگ [Barg] **Leaf**	پ پشه [Pasha] **Mosquito**	پ [To...] **Ball**	
ج جیب [Jayb] **Pocket**	چ چتر [Chatree] **Umbrella**	ح حلزون [Halzoon] **Snail**	خ خر [Khar] **Donkey**	درخت [Darakht] **Tree**	ذره بین [Zara been] **Magnifying Glass**
ر روباه [Rooba] **Fox**	ز زن [Zan] **Woman**	ژ ژرف [zharf] **Deep**	س سیب [Sayb] **Apple**	ش شتر [Shutur] **Camel**	ص صابون [Saaboon] **Soap**
ض امضا [Em-zaa] **Signature**	ط طلا [Tilaa] **Gold**	ظ ظهر [Zuhr] **Noon**	ع عینک [Aynak] **Glasses**	غ باغ [Baagh] **Garden**	ف فیل [Feel] **Elephant**
ق قیچی [Qaichee] **Scissors**	ک کتاب [Ketaab] **Book**	گ گل [Gul] **Flower**	ل لیمو [Leemoo] **Lemon**	م ماهی [Maahee] **Fish**	ن ناک [Naak] **Pear**
و ورزش [Warzish] **Sport**	ه خواهر [Khwaa-Har] **Sisters**	ی یخ [Yakh] **Ice**			

DARI ALPHABET

الفبای دری

© MamaLearn.com

An Introductory conversational DARI book for children

Hello

Salaam

سلام

What is your name

Naam-ā shoma chēst?

نام شما چیست؟

Hi. My name is Catherine

Salaam. Naamĕm kaatrin ast.

سالم. نامم کاترین است.

How are you doing?

chĕtor hastĕd?

چطور هستید؟

I'm fine, Thank you

man khob hastam, tashakor.

من خوب هستم، تشکر

Where are you from?

Šoma az kojā hasted?

شما از کجا هستید؟

I'm from California

man az kaliforniyaa hastam

‫من از ایالت کالیفرنیا هستم.‬

Nice to meet you.

Khoshaal Shodom az mulaqat e shuma.

خشحال شدم از ملاقات شما

Thank you

tashakor

تشکر

You're welcome.

kaabĕleš nĭst.

قابلش نیست

Good-bye

khodaa haafĕz

خدا حافظ

I can't speak Dari well

Ma dorost dari yad nadaraom

من درست دری یاد ندارم

? I don't understand

Mann namefahmam

من نمیفهیم

Do you speak English?

aya Shuma Englisi Yaad Daren?

آیا شما انگریسي یاد دارن؟

Is there someone here who speaks English?

Aaya da inja kase hast ke englisi yaad dashta basha ?

آیا انجا کس است که انگلیسي یاد داشته باشه؟

Open	Closed
baaz	basteh
باز	بسته

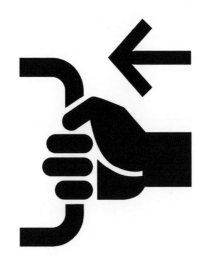

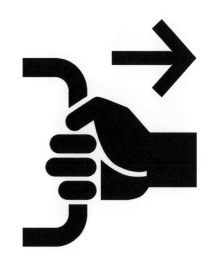

Push

Pull

feshar

kash

فشار

کش

Men

Women

mardan

zanan

مردان

زنان

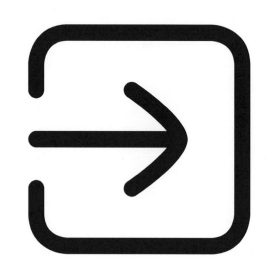

Entrance

dakhl

داخل

Exit

kharij

خارج

Yes

No

Baleh

Ne

بله

نه

Good Morning	Good Night
Sob bakhir	Shab bakhir
صبح بخير	شب بخير

Help!

Komak!

اكمک!

Look Out !

Sayhel ko!

اسيل كن!

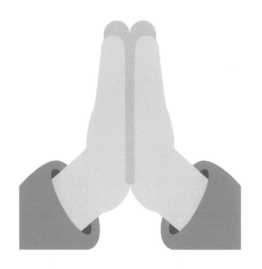

Please

I'm sorry

Lotfaan

Mazrat Mekhwaham

لطفا

محذرت میخواهم

Printed in Great Britain
by Amazon